WHO LIVES HERE?

FROZEN LANDS

Mary-Jane Wilkins

BROWN BEAR BOOKS

Published by Brown Bear Books Ltd
4877 N. Circulo Bujia
Tucson, AZ 85718
USA

and

First Floor
9–17 St Albans Place
London N1 0NX

ISBN 978-1-78121-347-6

Library of Congress Cataloging-in-Publication Data available on request

Picture Researcher: Clare Newman
Designer: Melissa Roskell
Design Manager: Keith Davis
Editorial Director: Lindsey Lowe
Children's Publisher: Anne O'Daly

Printed in China

Picture Credits
The photographs in this book are used by permission and through the courtesy of:

Front Cover: Shutterstock: Anita Andre tl, BMJ cl, Evgeny Kovalev main, Vladimir Melnik bl, Elena Shchipkova br;
Inside: 1, ©Shutterstock/Bike Rider London; 4, ©Shutterstock/Armin Rose; 4-5, ©Shutterstock/Elnavegante; 6, ©Shutterstock/Anita Andre; 6-7, ©Shutterstock/Florida Stock; 8, ©FLPA/Michio Hosino/Minden Pictures; 9, ©Shutterstock/BMJ; 10, ©FLPA/Samuel Blanc/Biosphoto; 10-11, ©Shutterstock/Volt Collection; 12, ©Shutterstock/Sylvie Bouchard; 12-13, © FLPA/T. W. P./Imagebroker; 14, ©Shutterstock/Cedric Weber; 14-15, ©FLPA/Hiroya Minakuchi/Minden Pictures; 16, ©FLPA/Sergey Gorshkov/Minden Pictures; 16-17, ©Shutterstock/Outdoorsman; 18, ©Thinkstock/Eva Pum/iStock; 19, ©Shutterstock/Tony Brindley; 20, ©Shutterstock/Jeff McGraw; 20-21, ©Shutterstock/Sergey Krasnoshchokov; 22, ©Shutterstock/Volodymyr Goinyk; 23, ©Shutterstock/Mikhail Kolesnikov.
T=Top, C=Center, B=Bottom, L=Left, R=Right

Brown Bear Books has made every attempt to contact the copyright holder. If you have any information please contact: licensing@brownbearbooks.co.uk

CONTENTS

Where Are the FROZEN LANDS?

The coldest places on Earth are the polar regions. The Arctic is in the far north of our planet. Most of it is ocean covered in ice.

Seals live in polar regions. They feed on the fish that swim in the icy seas.

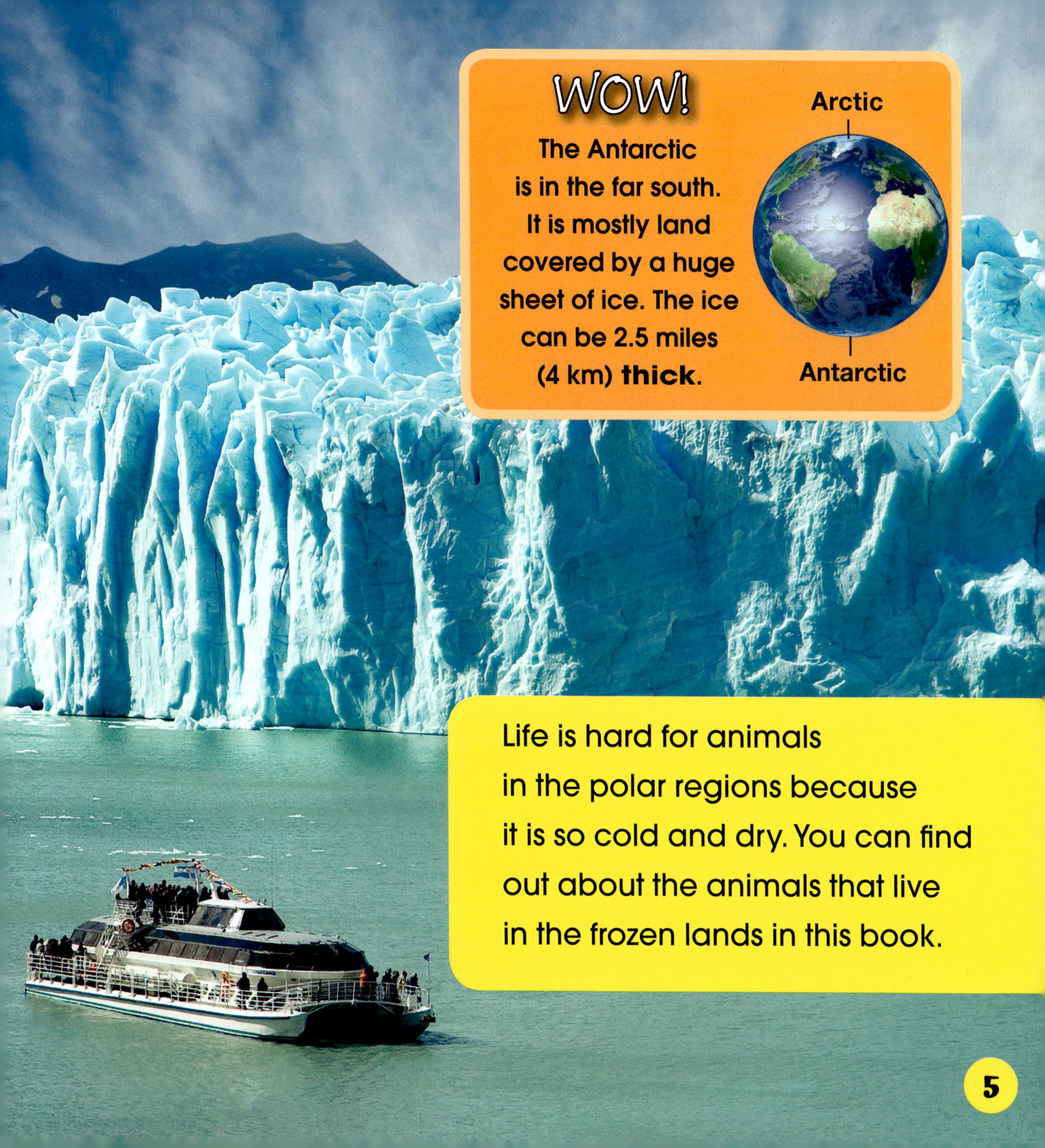

WOW!

The Antarctic is in the far south. It is mostly land covered by a huge sheet of ice. The ice can be 2.5 miles (4 km) **thick**.

Life is hard for animals in the polar regions because it is so cold and dry. You can find out about the animals that live in the frozen lands in this book.

POLAR BEAR

Polar bears live on the Arctic ice. Their **thick** fur keeps them warm and helps them blend in with the snow and ice.

WOW!

Polar bears have fur on the bottom of their paws.

These bears are strong swimmers. They are predators that hunt seals. A bear lies in wait at the edge of the ice. When a seal comes up for air the bear ***grabs*** its prey.

HARP SEAL

Harp seals spend most of their time swimming in the Arctic Ocean. They catch fish to eat. These seals can stay underwater for 15 minutes. Sharks, polar bears, and killer whales hunt them.

Baby harp seals have a fluffy white coat.

Walruses break holes in the ice with their tusks.

WALRUS

Huge walruses have lots of **blubber**. This is a thick layer of fat under the skin. It keeps the animal warm. A walrus also has tusks that can be 3 feet (1 m) long.

EMPEROR PENGUIN

The emperor penguin is the **biggest** penguin in the world. Most emperor penguins are about 43 inches (110 cm) tall.

The female penguin lays one egg a year. The male penguin looks after the egg until it hatches.

Emperor penguins live in Antarctica. They have **fat** bodies and layers of feathers. The penguins huddle together in big groups to keep warm.

MUSK OX

These big, shaggy animals live in the Arctic. Their **w i d e** hooves stop them sinking into the snow.

WOW!

A musk ox has the l o n g e s t hairs of any animal. They can be 2 feet (60 cm) long.

In winter, musk ox dig through the snow to find roots, moss, and lichen to eat. In summer, they eat flowers and grasses.

WHALES

The blue whale is the **biggest** animal on Earth. It can grow to be 110 feet (34 m) long and weigh more than **200 tons** (181 tonnes). Its tongue can weigh as much as an elephant!

White whales live in the Arctic Ocean. Whales live in groups called pods. They "talk" to each other in clicks and whistles.

Blue whales swim to the polar seas in summer to find food. They eat tiny shrimp called krill.

ARCTIC FOX

This fox turns white in winter. Its coat makes the fox hard to see in snow. In the summer, its coat turns brown or gray.

The Arctic fox eats lemmings, eggs, and birds. This fox is jumping on a lemming under the snow.

The Arctic fox has a bushy tail. It curls the tail around its body when it lies down.

LEMMING

This little animal is the size of a mouse. It has white fur in winter and brown fur in summer, like other Arctic animals.

Lemmings dig burrows to hide in. They eat plants and berries.

Arctic terns eat fish and sand eels.

ARCTIC TERN

This bird may fly **farther** than any bird in the world. In the winter it lives in the Antarctic. Then in May it flies north all the way to the Arctic. There it makes a nest and lays eggs.

CARIBOU

These big deer walk, or ***migrate***, hundreds of miles north every spring. Huge herds look for grasses and plants to eat. In the summer, a caribou eats 12 pounds (5.4 kg) of food a day.

A caribou's antlers can be 51 inches (130 cm) long.

As soon as snow begins to fall, the caribou set off south again. They may walk 3,100 miles (4,960 km) every year.

FROZEN LANDS FACTS

- The North Pole is the farthest north you can go on Earth. The sea ice is 6 feet (1.8 m) thick.
- The South Pole is the farthest south you can go. It is near the middle of the ice on Antarctica.
- Icebergs are huge blocks of ice that float in the polar oceans. They can be bigger than a house!
- In summer the Sun never sets near the poles. It is light all day and all night! But in winter it is dark all day.

USEFUL WORDS

lichen
A living thing that grows on rocks and dead wood.

migrate
To move to another place. Animals migrate to find food or have young.

predator
An animal that hunts other animals for food. The polar bear is a predator.

prey
An animal hunted and eaten by another animal. Seals are the prey of a polar bear.

FIND OUT MORE

Ice is Nice Bonnie Worth, Random House, 2010

Life Cycles: Polar Lands Sean Callery, Kingfisher, 2012

Polar Animal Adaptations Lisa J. Amstutz, Capstone Press, 2011

Polar Bears and Penguins Katharine Hall, Sylvan Dell Publishing, 2014

INDEX